I0167402

Kyrgyz Vocabulary:
A Kyrgyz Language Guide

Nurlan Akhmetov

Contents

List of Kyrgyz letters

Order	Kyrgyz Cyrillic alphabet	Kyrgyz Latin alphabet	IPA
01	А а	A a	/ɑ/
Example:	ат	at	/ɑt/
02	Б б	B b	/b/
Example:	бака	baka	/bɑkɑ/
03	В в	V v	/v/
Example:	ваза	vaza	/vɑzɑ/
04	Г г	G g	/g/
Example:	гезит	gezit	/gɛzit/
05	Д д	D d	/d/
Example:	дене	dene	/dɛnɛ/
06	Е е	E e	/ɛ/~/e/
Example:	Европа	Evropa	/ɛvropɑ/
07	Ё ё	Yo yo	/jo/
Example:	коён	koyon	/qojon/
08	Ж ж	J j	/d͡ʒ/
Example:	жука	juka	/d͡ʒuqɑ/
09	З з	Z z	/z/
Example:	зыкым	zykym	/zɨqɨm/
10	И и	I i	/i/
Example:	ит	it	/it/
11	Й й	Yi yi	/j/
Example:	кайгы	kayigy	/qɑj gɨ/
12	К к	K k	/q/~/k/
Example:	көркөм	körköm	/kørkøm/
13	Л л	L l	/l/~/ʎ/
Example:	белги	belgi	/bɛlgi/
14	М м	M m	/m/
Example:	мышык	myshyk	/mɨʃɨq/
15	Н н	N n	/n/
Example:	нан	nan	/nɑn/
16	Ң ң	Ng ng	/ŋ/
Example:	жаңгак	jangak	/d͡ʒɑŋɑq/

17	О о	O o	/o/
Example:	обон	obon	/obon/
18	Ѳ ѳ	Ö ö	/ø/
Example:	ѳмүр	ömür	/ømyr/
19	П п	P p	/p/
Example:	карапа	karapa	/qɑrɑpɑ/
20	Р р	R r	/r/
Example:	аракет	araket	/ɑrɑqɛt/
21	С с	S s	/s/
Example:	саат	saat	/sɑːt/
22	Т т	T t	/t/
Example:	таш	tash	/tɑʃ/
23	У у	U u	/u/
Example:	убай	ubayi	/ubɑj/
24	Ү ү	Ü ü	/y/
Example:	үкү	ükü	/yky/
25	Ф ф	F f	/f/
Example:	фонтан	fontan	/fontɑn/
26	Х х	H h	/h/
Example:	халва	halva	/hɑlvɑ/
27	Ц ц	Tz tz	/ʦ/
Example:	цирк	tzirk	/ʦirk/
28	Ч ч	Ch ch	/ʧ/
Example:	чайнек	chayinek	/ʧɑjnɛk/
29	Ш ш	Sh sh	/ʃ/
Example:	шакек	shakek	/ʃɑkɛk/
30	Щ щ	Sh' sh'	/ɕ/
Example:	плащ	plash'	/plɑɕ/
31	ь	'	/ʲ/~/'/
Example:	июнь	iiun'	/ijunʲ/
32	Ы ы	Y y	/ɨ/
Example:	ыр	yr	/ɨr/
33	ъ	"	-
Example:	адъютант	ad"iutant	/ɑd"jutɑnt/
34	Э э	E e	/ɛ/
Example:	эмен	emen	/ɛmɛn/

35	Ю ю	Iu iu	/ju/
Example:	кюн	kuiun	/qujun/
36	Я я	Ya ya	/ja/
Example:	таяк	tayak	/tɑjɑq/

1) Measurements
1) Өлчөө бирдиктери
1) Ölchöö birdikteri

acre

акр

akr

---

centimeter

сантим**е**тр

santimetr

Cup

кес**е**

kese

---

degree

гр**а**дус

gradus

---

depth

тере**ң**д**и**к

terengdik

---

dozen

он эки

on eki

---

foot

фут

fut

---

gallon

галлон

gallon

---

gram

грамм

gramm

---

height

бийиктик

biyiiktik

---

inch

дюйм

diuyim

---

kilometer

километр

kilometr

length

узундук

uzunduk

liter

литр

litr

meter

метр

metr

mile

миля

milya

minute

мүнөт

münöt

ounce

унция

untziya

perimeter

периметр

perimetr

pint

пинта

pinta

pound

фунт

funt

quart

кварта

kvarta

ruler

сызгыч

syzgych

scale

масштаб

masshtab

small

кичинекей

kichinekeyi

tablespoon

чоң кашык

chong kashyk

teaspoon

чай кашык

chayi kashyk

ton

тонна

tonna

volume

көлөм

kölöm

weight

салмак

salmak

---

width

кеңдик

kengdik

---

yard

ярд

yard

Time

Убакыт

Ubakyt

What time is it?

Саат канча болду?

Saat kancha boldu?

It's 1:00 AM/PM

Саат түшкө чейинки/түштөн кийинки 1:00 болду

Saat tüshkö cheyiinki/tüshtön kiyiinki 1:00 boldu

It's 2:00 AM/PM

Саат түшкө чейинки/түштөн кийинки 2:00 болду

Saat tüshkö cheyiinki/tüshtön kiyiinki 2:00 boldu

It's 3:00 AM/PM

Саат түшкө чейинки/түштөн кийинки 3:00 болду

Saat tüshkö cheyiinki/tüshtön kiyiinki 3:00 boldu

It's 4:00 AM/PM

Саат түшкө чейинки/түштөн кийинки 4:00 болду

Saat tüshkö cheyiinki/tüshtön kiyiinki 4:00 boldu

It's 5:00 AM/PM

Саат түшкө чейинки/түштөн кийинки 5:00 болду

Saat tüshkö cheyiinki/tüshtön kiyiinki 5:00 boldu

It's 6:00 AM/PM

Саат түшкө чейинки/түштөн кийинки 6:00 болду

Saat tüshkö cheyiinki/tüshtön kiyiinki 6:00 boldu

It's 7:00 AM/PM

Саат түшкө чейинки/түштөн кийинки 7:00 болду

Saat tüshkö cheyiinki/tüshtön kiyiinki 7:00 boldu

It's 8:00 AM/PM

Саат түшкө чейинки/түштөн кийинки 8:00 болду

Saat tüshkö cheyiinki/tüshtön kiyiinki 8:00 boldu

It's 9:00 AM/PM

Саат түшкө чейинки/түштөн кийинки 9:00 болду

Saat tüshkö cheyiinki/tüshtön kiyiinki 9:00 boldu

It's 10:00 AM/PM

Саат түшкө чейинки/түштөн кийинки 10:00 болду

Saat tüshkö cheyiinki/tüshtön kiyiinki 10:00 boldu

It's 11:00 AM/PM

Саат түшкө чейинки/түштөн кийинки 11:00 болду

Saat tüshkö cheyiinki/tüshtön kiyiinki 11:00 boldu

It's 12:00 AM/PM

Саат түшкө чейинки/түштөн кийинки 12:00 болду

Saat tüshkö cheyiinki/tüshtön kiyiinki 12:00 boldu

---

in the morning

эртең менен

erteng menen

---

in the afternoon

түштө

tüshtö

---

in the evening

кечкурун

kechkurun

---

at night

түндө

tündö

---

afternoon

чак түш

chak tüsh

---

annual

ЖЫЛДЫК

jyldyk

calendar

календарь/күнбарак

kalendar'/künbarak

daytime

КҮНДҮЗ

kündüz

decade

ОН ЖЫЛДЫК

on jyldyk

evening

кечкурун

kechkurun

hour

саат

saat

midnight

түн ортосу

tün ortosu

---

minute

мүнөт

münöt

---

morning

таң

tang

---

month

ай

ayi

---

noon

түш

tüsh

---

now

азыр

azyr

---

o'clock

саат

saat

---

past

өттү

öttü

---

present

азыркы маал/учур чак

azyrky maal/uchur chak

---

second

секунда

sekunda

---

sunrise

таӊ атуу

tang atuu

---

sunset

күн батуу

kün batuu

today

бүгүн

bügün

tonight

бүгүн кечинде

bügün kechinde

tomorrow

эртең

erteng

week

апта

apta

year

жыл

jyl

yesterday

кечээ

kechee

Months of the Year

Жылдын айлары

Jyldyn ayilary

January

Үчтүн айы

Üchtün ayiy

February

Бирдин айы

Birdin ayiy

March

Жалган куран

Jalgan kuran

April

Чын куран

Chyn kuran

May

Бугу

Bugu

June

Кулжа

Kulja

July

Теке

Teke

August

Баш оона

Bash oona

September

Аяк оона

Ayak oona

October

Тогуздун айы

Toguzdun ayiy

November

Жетинин айы

Jetinin ayiy

December

Бештин айы

Beshtin ayiy

Days of the Week

Аптанын күндөрү

Aptanyn kündörü

Monday

Дүйшөмбү

Düyishömbü

Tuesday

Шейшемби

Sheyishembi

Wednesday

Шаршемби

Sharshembi

Thursday

Бейшемби

Beyishembi

Friday

Жума

Juma

Saturday

Ишемби

Ishembi

Sunday

Жекшемби

Jekshembi

Seasons

Жыл мезгилдери

Jyl mezgilderi

winter

кыш

kysh

spring

жаз

jaz

summer

жай

jayi

fall/autumn

күз

küz

Numbers

Сандар

Sandar

One(1)

Бир(1)

Bir(1)

Two(2)

Эки(2)

Eki(2)

Three(3)

Үч(3)

Üch(3)

Four(4)

Төрт(4)

Tört(4)

Five(5)

Беш(5)

Besh(5)

Six(6)

Алты(6)

Alty(6)

Seven(7)

Жети(7)

Jeti(7)

Eight(8)

Сегиз(8)

Segiz(8)

Nine(9)

Тогуз(9)

Toguz(9)

Ten(10)

Он(10)

On(10)

Eleven(11)

Он бир(11)

On bir(11)

Twelve(12)

Он эки(12)

On eki(12)

Twenty(20)

Жыйырма(20)

Jyyiyrma(20)

Fifty(50)

Элүү(50)

Elüü(50)

Hundred(100)

Жүз(100)

Jüz(100)

Thousand(1000)

Мин(1000)

Ming(1000)

Ten Thousand(10,000)

Он мин(10,000)

On ming(10,000)

Hundred Thousand(100,000)

Жүз мин(100,000)

Jüz ming(100,000)

Million(1,000,000)

Миллион(1,000,000)

Million(1,000,000)

Billion(1,000,000,000)

Миллиард(1,000,000,000)

Milliard(1,000,000,000)

Ordinal Numbers

Иреттик сандар

Irettik sandar

first

бири**и**

birinchi

second

экинчи

ekinchi

third

үчүнчү

üchünchü

fourth

төртүнчү

törtünchü

fifth

бешинчи

beshinchi

sixth

алтынч**ы**

altynchy

seventh

жетинч**и**

jetinchi

eighth

сегизинч**и**

segizinchi

ninth

тогузунч**у**

toguzunchu

tenth

онунч**у**

onunchu

twentieth

жыйырманч**ы**

jyyiyrmanchy

twenty-first

жыйырма биринчи

jyyiyrma birinchi

hundredth

жүзүнчү

jüzünchü

thousandth

миӊинчи

minginchi

millionth

миллионунчу

millionunchu

billionth

миллиардынчы

milliardynchy

Geometric Shapes

Геометриялык фигуралар

Geometriyalyk figuralar

circle

айлана

ayilana

---

heart

жүрөк

jürök

---

line

сызык

syzyk

---

octagon

сегиз бурчтук

segiz burchtuk

---

oval

узунча тегерек

uzuncha tegerek

---

parallel

параллель

parallel'

pentagon

беш бурчтук

besh burchtuk

perpendicular

перпендикуляр

perpendikulyar

polygon

көп бурчтук

köp burchtuk

rectangle

тик бурчтук

tik burchtuk

square

квадрат

kvadrat

star

ЖЫЛД**Ы**З

jyldyz

triangle

үч бурчт**у**к

üch burchtuk

Colors

Түстөр

Tüstör

black

кар**а**

kara

blue

көк

kök

brown

күр**ө**ң

küröng

gray

боз

boz

---

green

жашыл

jashyl

---

navy blue

күңүрт көк

küngürt kök

---

orange

саргыч

sargych

---

pink

кызгылт

kyzgylt

---

purple

кызгылт көгүш

kyzgylt kögüsh

---

red

кызыл

kyzyl

---

silver

күмүш

kümüsh

---

white

ак

ak

---

yellow

сары

sary

Related Verbs

Тиешелүү этиштер

Tieshelüü etishter

to add

кошуу

koshuu

---

to change

өзгөртүү

özgörtüü

to check

текшерүү

teksherüü

to color

боё

boyo

to count

эсептөө

eseptöö

to divide

бөлүү

bölüü

to figure

сүрөттөө

süröttöö

to fill

толтуруу

tolturuu

to guess

божомолдоо

bojomoldoo

to measure

ченөө

chenöö

to multiply

көбөйтүү

köböyitüü

to subtract

кемитүү

kemitüü

to take

алуу

aluu

to tell time

саатт** ы** айту**у**

*saatt**y** ayitu**u***

---

to verify

ырасто**о**

*yrasto**o***

---

to watch

байко**о** жүргүзү**ү**

*bayiko**o** jürgüzü**ü***

---

2) Weather
2) Аба ырайы
2) Aba yrayiy

air

аб**а**

*ab**a***

---

atmosphere

атмосфер**а**

*atmosfer**a***

---

blizzard

бурган**ак**

*burgan**ak***

---

breeze

жел

jel

---

climate

клим**ат**

*klim**at***

---

cloud

булут

bulut

cold

суук

suuk

cyclone

циклон

tziklon

degree

градус

gradus

depression

төмөн басымдуулук

tömön basymduuluk

dew

шүүдүрүм

shüüdürüm

dry

кургак

kurgak

flood

ташкын

tashkyn

fog

туман

tuman

forecast

прогноз

prognoz

freeze

үшүк

üshük

frost

кыроо

kyroo

hail

мөндүр

möndür

heat

ысык

ysyk

high

жогору

jogoru

humidity

нымдуулук

nymduuluk

hurricane

бороон

boroon

ice

муз

muz

lightning

чагылган

chagylgan

low

төмөн

tömön

meteorology

метеорология

meteorologiya

outlook

сереп

serep

overcast

күн бүркөк

kün bürkök

precipitation

жаан-чачын

jaan-chachyn

pressure

басым

basym

---

radar

локатор

lokator

---

rain

жаан

jaan

---

snow

кар

kar

---

storm

бороон-чапкын

boroon-chapkyn

---

temperature

температура

temperatura

---

thermal

жогору кеткен агым

jogoru ketken agym

thermometer

термометр

termometr

thunder

күн күркүрөө

kün kürküröö

tornado

куюн

kuiun

tropical storm

тропиктик бороон

tropiktik boroon

warm

жылуу

jyluu

weather

аба ырайы

aba yrayiy

weather report

аба ырайы боюнча маалымат

aba yrayiy boiuncha maalymat

wind

шамал

shamal

wind chill

шамалдап муздоо

shamaldap muzdoo

Related Verbs

Тиешелүү этиштер
Tieshelüü etishter

to cool down

муздоо

muzdoo

to drizzle

себелөө

sebelöö

to feel

сезилүү/сезүү

sezilüü/sezüü

to forecast

алдын ала айтуу

aldyn ala ayituu

to hail

мөндүрдүн жаашы

möndürdün jaashy

to rain

жамгырдын жаашы

jamgyrdyn jaashy

to shine

күндүн ачык болуусу

kündün achyk boluusu

to snow

кард**ы**н жа**а**шы

kardyn jaashy

to storm

бороонд**у**н болуш**у**

boroondun bolushu

to watch

байко**о** ж**ү**рг**ү**з**ү**

bayikoo jürgüzüü

3) **People**
3) Адамдар
3) Adamdar

athlete

спортчу

sportchu

---

boy

бала

bala

---

brother

бир тууган/ага/байке/ини

bir tuugan/aga/bayike/ini

---

brother-in-law

кайын ага/кайын ини

kayiyn aga/kayiyn ini

---

businessman

бизнесмен

biznesmen

---

candidate

кандидат

kandidat

child/children

бала/балдар

bala/baldar

coach

тренер/репетитор/коуч

trener/repetitor/kouch

cousin

бир тууган/аталаш бир тууган

bir tuugan/atalash bir tuugan

daughter

кыз

kyz

daughter-in-law

келин

kelin

driver

айдоочу/шофёр

ayidoochu/shofyor

family

үй бүлө

üyi bülö

farmer

фермер

fermer

father/dad

ата

ata

father-in-law

кайын ата/кайната

kayiyn ata/kayinata

friend

дос/курбу/жолдош

dos/kurbu/joldosh

girl

кыз

kyz

---

grandchildren

неберел**е**р

nebereler

---

granddaughter

небер**е**/кыз небер**е**/жээн небер**е**

nebere/kyz nebere/jeen nebere

---

grandfather

чоң ат**а**

chong ata

---

grandmother

чоң эн**е**/чоң ап**а**

chong ene/chong apa

---

grandson

небер**е**/уул небер**е**/жээн небер**е**

nebere/uul nebere/jeen nebere

husband

күйөө/жолдош

küyiöö/joldosh

---

kid

бала/бөбөк

bala/böbök

---

man

эркек киши

erkek kishi

---

mother/mom

апа/эне

apa/ene

---

mother-in-law

кайын эне/кайнене

kayiyn ene/kayinene

---

nephew

ини/жээн

ini/jeen

---

niece

карындаш/жээн

karyndash/jeen

---

parent

ата/эне

ata/ene

---

sister

эже/синди/карындаш

eje/singdi/karyndash

---

sister-in-law

жеңе/келин/балдыз/кайын эже/кайын синди

jenge/kelin/baldyz/kayiyn eje/kayiyn singdi

---

son

уул/бала

uul/bala

---

son-in-law

күйөө бала

küyöö bala

---

student

студент/окуучу

student/okuuchu

teenager

жаш бала/жаш кыз

jash bala/jash kyz

tourist

турист

turist

wife

аял/жолдош/катын/жубай

ayal/joldosh/katyn/jubayi

woman

аял/аял киши

ayal/ayal kishi

Characteristics

Сүрөтөө
Sürötöö

attractive

жагымдуу/жакшынакай

jagymduu/jakshynakayi

---

beautiful

сулуу

suluu

---

black hair

кара чач

kara chach

---

blind

сокур

sokur

---

blond

ак саргыл

ak sargyl

blue eyes

көк көз

kök köz

brown eyes

кой көз/күрөң көз

koyi köz/küröng köz

brown hair/brunette

күрөң чач/брюнет

küröng chach/briunet

deaf

дүлөй

dülöyi

divorced

ажырашкан

ajyrashkan

fat

толук

toluk

gray hair

ак чач

ak chach

---

green eyes

көк көз

kök köz

---

handsome

нуру төгүлгөн

nuru tögülgön

---

hazel eyes

кой көз

koyi köz

---

married

үйлөнгөн/турмушка чыккан

üyilöngön/turmushka chykkan

---

mustache

мурут

murut

---

old

кар**ы**/картаң

kary/kartang

petite

жапалд**а**ш

japaldash

plump

тол**у**к

toluk

pregnant

кош бойлу**у**/боюнд**а** бар

kosh boyiluu/boiunda bar

red head

кыз**ы**л чач

kyzyl chach

short

жапалд**а**ш

japaldash

short hair

кыска чач

kyska chach

---

skinny

жука

juka

---

stocky

чымыр

chymyr

---

tall

узун бойлуу/узун/бойлуу

uzun boyiluu/uzun/boyiluu

---

thin

арык/арыкчырай

aryk/arykchyrayi

---

young

жаш

jash

Stages of Life

Жашоо этаптары
Jashoo etaptary

adolescence

жаштык/улан жаштык

jashtyk/ulan jashtyk

---

adult

бойго жеткендик

boyigo jetkendik

---

anniversary

маараке

maarake

---

birth

төрөлүү

törölüü

---

death

өлүм

ölüm

---

divorce

ажырашуу

ajyrashuu

graduation

окууну аяктоо

okuunu ayaktoo

infant

ымыркай/бөбөк/бала/наристе

ymyrkayi/böbök/bala/nariste

marriage

үйлөнүү

üyilönüü

middle-aged

орто жашар

orto jashar

newborn

жаңы төрөлгөн бала

jangy törölgön bala

preschooler

мектепке чейинки бала

mektepke cheyiinki bala

preteen

онго чыга элек бала

ongo chyga elek bala

senior citizen

улгайган адам

ulgayigan adam

teenager

жаш бала/жаш кыз/улан жашар адам

jash bala/jash kyz/ulan jashar adam

toddler

ымыркай/бөбөк/бала/наристе

ymyrkayi/böbök/bala/nariste

young adult

жашы толгон адам

jashy tolgon adam

Religion

Дин/Религия

Din/Religiya

Atheist/Agnostic

Атеист/Агностик

Ateist/Agnostik

Buddhist

Буддист

Buddist

Christian

Христиан

Hristian

Hindu

Индуист

Induist

Jewish

Иудей

Iudeyi

Muslim

Мусулман

Musulman

Sikh

Сикх

Sikh

Work

Жумуш

Jumush

accountant

бухгалтер

buhgalter

associate

жумушчу/өнөк/партнёр

jumushchu/önök/partnyor

astronaut

космонавт/астронавт

kosmonavt/astronavt

banker

банкир

bankir

---

carpenter

жыгач уста

jygach usta

---

chef

ашпозчу/башкы ашпозчу

ashpozchu/bashky ashpozchu

---

clerk

клерк/кеңсе жумушчусу

klerk/kengse jumushchusu

---

custodian

кароолчу/сактоочу/көзөмөлдөөчү

karoolchu/saktoochu/közömöldööchü

---

dentist

стоматолог/дантист/тиш доктур

stomatolog/dantist/tish doktur

---

doctor

доктур

doktur

electrician

электрик

elektrik

executive

башкарма/директор

bashkarma/direktor

judge

сот

sot

lawyer

адвокат

advokat

librarian

китепканачы

kitepkanachy

manager

менежер

menejer

pharmacist

фармацевт

farmatzevt

pilot

пилот

pilot

policeman

полиция кызматкери

politziya kyzmatkeri

preacher

дин кызматкери

din kyzmatkeri

president

президент

prezident

representative

өкүлдөр палатасынын мүчөсү/өкүл

öküldör palatasynyn müchösü/ökül

scientist

окмуштуу

okmushtuu

secretary

катчы

katchy

soldier

солдат

soldat

teacher

мугалим/окутуучу

mugalim/okutuuchu

technician

техник

tehnik

treasurer

кассир

kassir

writer

жазуучу

jazuuchu

zoologist

зоолог

zoolog

Related Verbs

Тиешелүү этиштер
Tieshelüü etishter

to grow

өсүү

ösüü

to love

сүйүү

süyiüü

to make

жасоо/кылуу/өбөлгө түзүү

jasoo/kyluu/öbölgö tüzüü

---

to manage

башкаруу/алы жетүү/колунан келүү

bashkaruu/aly jetüü/kolunan kelüü

---

to serve

кызмат кылуу/пайда келтирүү

kyzmat kyluu/payida keltirüü

---

to talk

сүйлөшүү/айтуу

süyilöshüü/ayituu

---

to think

ойлонуу

oyilonuu

---

to work

иштөө

ishtöö

---

to worship

сыйынуу/баш ийүү

syyiynuu/bash iyiüü

4) Parts of the Body
4) Дене мүчөлөрү
4) Dene müchölörü

arm

кол

kol

back

арка

arka

belly

курсак/ич

kursak/ich

blood

кан

kan

bone

сөөк

söök

brain

мээ

mee

---

breast

эмчек

emchek

---

buttocks

жамбаш

jambash

---

cheek

жаак/бет

jaak/bet

---

chest

төш

tösh

---

ear

кулак

kulak

---

eye

көз

köz

---

face

бет

bet

---

finger

манжа

manja

---

foot/feet

бут

but

---

hair

чач

chach

---

hand

ченгел

chenggel

---

head

баш

bash

heart

жүрөк

jürök

knee

тизе

tize

leg

бут

but

lips

эриндер

erinder

mouth

ооз

ooz

muscle

булчуң

bulchung

nail

тырмак

tyrmak

neck

моюн

moiun

nose

мурун

murun

shoulder

ийин

iyiin

skin

тери

teri

stomach

аш-казан/карын

ash-kazan/karyn

teeth/tooth

тиш

tish

tongue

тил

til

Related Verbs

Тиешелүү этиштер
Tieshelüü etishter

to exercise

машыгуу/чыңоо

mashyguu/chyngoo

to feel

сезүү

sezüü

to hear

угуу

uguu

to see

көрүү

körüü

to smell

жыттоо/жыт сезүү/жыттануу

jyttoo/jyt sezüü/jyttanuu

to taste

даам сезүү/даамдануу

daam sezüü/daamdanuu

to touch

тийүү/козгоо

tiyiüü/kozgoo

5) Animals
5) Жаныбарлар
5) Janybarlar

alligator

аллигатор

alligator

---

bat

жарганат

jarganat

---

bear

аюу

aiuu

---

cat

мышык

myshyk

---

cougar

пантера

pantera

---

cow

уй

uyi

crocodile

крокодил

krokodil

deer

бугу

bugu

dinosaur

динозавр

dinozavr

dog

ит

it

elephant

пил

pil

fox

түлкү

tülkü

frog

бака

baka

giraffe

жираф

jiraf

goat

эчки

echki

hippopotamus

бегемот

begemot

horse

ат

at

iguana

игуана

iguana

---

kangaroo

кенгуру

kenguru

---

lion

арстан

arstan

---

lizard

кескелдирик

keskeldirik

---

mouse

чычкан

chychkan

---

monkey

маймыл

mayimyl

---

otter

кундуз

kunduz

panda

панда

panda

pig

чочко

chochko

rabbit

коён

koyon

sheep

кой

koyi

snake

жылан

jylan

squirrel

тыйын чычкан

tyyiyn chychkan

tiger

жолборс

jolbors

turtle

таш бака

tash baka

wolf

карышкыр/бөрү

karyshkyr/börü

zebra

зебра

zebra

Birds

Канаттуулар
Kanattuular

chicken

жөжө

jöjö

crow

карга

karga

dove

көгүчкөн/ак көгүчкөн

kögüchkön/ak kögüchkön

duck

өрдөк

ördök

eagle

бүркүт

bürküt

flamingo

фламинго

flamingo

---

goose

каз

kaz

---

hawk

карчыга

karchyga

---

hummingbird

колибри

kolibri

---

owl

үкү

ükü

---

parrot

тоту куш

totu kush

---

pigeon

көгүчкөн

kögüchkön

rooster

короз

koroz

swan

ак куу

ak kuu

turkey

күрп/үндүк

kürp/ündük

Water/Ocean/Beach

Суу/Океан/Кум жээк

Suu/Okean/Kum jeek

catfish

ит балык/жаян

it balyk/jayan

crab

краб

krab

goldfish

алтын балык

altyn balyk

jellyfish

медуза

meduza

lobster

омар

omar

oyster

устрица

ustritza

salmon

лосось/сёмга

losos'/syomga

shark

акула

akula

tuna

туна/тунец

tuna/tunetz

whale

кит

kit

Insects

Курт-кумурскалар
Kurt-kumurskalar

ant

кумурска

kumurska

bee

аары

aary

beetle

коңуз

konguz

butterfly

көпөлөк

köpölök

earthworm

сөөлжан

sööljan

flea

бүргө

bürgö

fly

чымын

chymyn

gnat

майда чиркей

mayida chirkeyi

grasshopper

чегиртке

chegirtke

ladybug

эл кайда көчөт

el kayida köchöt

moth

күбө

kübö

mosquito

чиркей

chirkeyi

spider

жөргөмүш

jörgömüsh

wasp

аары/жапайы аары

aary/japayiy aary

Related Verbs

Тиешелүү этиштер
Tieshelüü etishter

to chase

кубалоо/уулоо/артынан түшүү
kubaloo/uuloo/artynan tüshüü

---

to feed

багуу/тамак берүү/жем берүү/тойгузуу
baguu/tamak berüü/jem berüü/toyiguzuu

---

to hibernate

чээнге кирүү
cheenge kirüü

---

to hunt

уулоо/мергенчилөө
uuloo/mergenchilöö

---

to move

жылуу
jyluu

---

to perch

конуу

konuu

to prey

кармап алуу/алуу/илүү

karmap aluu/aluu/ilüü

to run

чуркоо

churkoo

to swim

сүзүү

süzüü

to walk

басуу

basuu

6) Plants and Trees
6) Өсүмдүктөр жана дарактар
6) Ösümdüktör jana daraktar

bamboo

бамбук

bambuk

---

bean

буурчак

buurchak

---

berry

жемиш

jemish

---

blossom

гүл

gül

---

branch

бутак

butak

---

bulb

баш

bash

---

bush

бадал

badal

---

cactus

кактус

kaktus

---

carnation

гвоздика

gvozdika

---

corn

жүгөрү

jügörü

---

eucalyptus

эвкалипт

evkalipt

---

evergreen

дайыма көгөрүп туруучу

dayiyma kögörüp turuuchu

fern

папоротник

paporotnik

fertilizer

жер семирткич

jer semirtkich

flower

гүл

gül

forest

токой

tokoyi

fruit

мөмө/жемиш/мөмө-жемиш

mömö/jemish/mömö-jemish

garden

бак/короо/бакча

bak/koroo/bakcha

---

grain

дан

dan

---

grass

чөп

chöp

---

hay

чөп

chöp

---

herb

дары чөп

dary chöp

---

ivy

чырмоок

chyrmook

leaf

жалбырак

jalbyrak

lettuce

латук

latuk

lily

лилия

liliya

moss

мох

moh

nut

жаңгак

janggak

oak

эмен

emen

pine cone

тобурчак

toburchak

pine tree

кызыл карагай

kyzyl karagayi

plant

өсүмдүк

ösümdük

petal

желекче

jelekche

poison ivy

уулуу сумах

uuluu sumah

pollen

чаңча

changcha

pumpkin

ашкабак

ashkabak

root

там**ы**р

tamyr

roses

р**о**за бадал**ы**

roza badaly

sap

шир**e**

shire

seed

ур**у**к

uruk

shrub

бадал

badal

soil

жер/топурак

jer/topurak

---

stem

сабак

sabak

---

thorn

тикен

tiken

---

tree

дарак

darak

---

trunk

сөңгөк

sönggök

---

weed

отоо чөп

otoo chöp

Related Verbs

Тиешелүү этиштер

Tieshelüü etishter

to fertilize

жер семиртүү

jer semirtüü

to gather

чогултуу

chogultuu

to grow

өстүрүү

östürüü

to harvest

жыйноо

jyyinoo

to pick

терүү

terüü

to plant

тигүү

tigüü

to plow

жер айдоо

jer ayidoo

to rake

тырмооктоо/тырмоо

tyrmooktoo/tyrmoo

to sow

себүү

sebüü

to water

сугаруу

sugaruu

to weed

отоо

otoo

7) **Meeting Each Other**
7) Кезигишүү
7) Kezigishüü

Greetings/Introductions:
Саламдашуу/Таанышуу:
Salamdashuu/Taanyshuu:

Good morning

Кутмандуу таң

Kutmanduu tang

Good afternoon

Куттуу күн/Саламатсызбы

Kuttuu kün/Salamatsyzby

Good evening

Кутмандуу кеч

Kutmanduu kech

Good night

Түнүңүз бейпил болсун

Tününgüz beyipil bolsun

Hi

Салам

Salam

Hello

Саламатсызбы

Salamatsyzby

Have you met (name)?

(Кишинин аты) менен жолуктуңузбу?

(Kishinin aty) menen joluktunguzbu?

How are you?

Кандайсыз?

Kandayisyz?

How are you today?

Кандайсыз?

Kandayisyz?

How do you do?

Иштериңиз кандай?

Ishteringiz kandayi?

How's it going?

Иштер кандай?

Ishter kandayi?

I am (name).

Менин атым (кишинин аты).

Menin atym (kishinin aty).

It's nice to meet you.

Таанышканыма кубанычтамын.

Taanyshkanyma kubanychtamyn.

Meet (name).

(Кишинин аты) менен таанышып алыңыз.

(Kishinin aty) menen taanyshyp alyngyz.

My friends call me (nickname).

Досторум мени (кишинин каймана аты) деп аташат.

Dostorum meni (kishinin kayimana aty) dep atashat.

My name is (name).

Менин атым (кишинин аты).

Menin atym (kishinin aty).

Nice to see you again.

Кайрадан кезиккениме кубанычтамын.

Kayiradan kezikkenime kubanychtamyn.

Pleased to meet you.

Таанышканыма кубанычтамын.

Taanyshkanyma kubanychtamyn.

This is (name)

Бул (кишинин аты)

Bul (kishinin aty)

What's your name?

Атыңыз ким?

Atyngyz kim?

Who are you?

Сиз кимсиз?/Сиз ким болуп иштейсиз?

Siz kimsiz?/Siz kim bolup ishteyisiz?

Greeting Answers

Саламдашууга жооптор
Salamdashuuga jooptor

Fine, thanks.

Жакшы, алкыш./Жакшы, рахмат.
Jakshy, alkysh./Jakshy, rahmat.

I'm okay.

Жакшы эле жүрөм.
Jakshy ele jüröm.

I'm sick.

Ооруп жатам.
Oorup jatam.

I'm tired.

Чарчап турам.
Charchap turam.

Not too bad.

Өтө жаман эмес.
Ötö jaman emes.

Very well.

Абдан жакшы.

Abdan jakshy.

Saying Goodbye
Коштошуу
Koshtoshuu

Bye

Жакшы барыңыз

Jakshy baryngyz

Goodbye

Жакшы барыңыз

Jakshy baryngyz

Good night

Түнүңүз бейпил болсун

Tününgüz beyipil bolsun

See you later

Көрүшкөнчө

Körüshkönchö

See you soon

Көрүшкөнчө

Körüshkönchö

See you tomorrow

Эртең көрүшкөнчө

Erteng körüshkönchö

Courtesy

Сылыктык

Sylyktyk

Excuse me

Кечиресиз

Kechiresiz

Pardon me

Кечиресиз

Kechiresiz

I'm sorry

Кечирип коюңузчу

Kechirip koiunguzchu

Thanks

Алкыш/Рахмат

Alkysh/Rahmat

Thank you

Алкыш/Рахмат

Alkysh/Rahmat

You're welcome

Эч нерсе эмес

Ech nerse emes

Special Greetings

Куттуктоолор

Kuttuktoolor

Congratulations

Куттуктайм

Kuttuktayim

Get well soon

Тезирээк сакайып кетиңиз

Tezireek sakayiyp ketingiz

Good luck

Ийгилик каалайм

Iyigilik kaalayim

Happy New Year

Жаңы жылыңыз менен

Jangy jylyngyz menen

Happy Easter

Пасха майрамыңыз кут болсун

Paskha mayiramyngyz kut bolsun

Merry Christmas

Рождество майрамыңыз кут болсун

Rojdestvo mayiramyngyz kut bolsun

Well done

Азаматсыз

Azamatsyz

Related Verbs

Тиешелүү этиштер

Tieshelüü etishter

to greet

куттукто**о**

*kuttukto**o***

---

to meet

тосу**у**/жолугушу**у**

*tosu**u**/jolugushu**u***

---

to say

айту**у**

*ayitu**u***

---

to shake hands

кол алышу**у**

*kol alyshu**u***

---

to talk

сүйлөшү**ү**

*süyilöshü**ü***

---

to thank

алк**ы**ш айт**уу**/рахм**а**т айт**уу**

alkysh ayituu/rahmat ayituu

8) House
8) Үй
8) Üyi

appliances

тиричилик буюмдары

tirichilik buiumdary

---

attic

чатыр асты/чердак

chatyr asty/cherdak

---

backyard

короо

koroo

---

balcony

балкон

balkon

---

basement

түпкү бөлмө

tüpkü bölmö

---

bathroom

ванна бөлмөсү

vanna bölmösü

bed

керебет/төшөк

kerebet/töshök

bedroom

уйку бөлмөсү

uyiku bölmösü

bookshelf/bookcase

китеп текчеси/китеп үкөгү/китеп шкафы

kitep tekchesi/kitep ükögü/kitep shkafy

cabinet

үкөк/комод/шкаф

ükök/komod/shkaf

carpet

килем

kilem

carport

унаа чатыры

unaa chatyry

ceiling

шып

shyp

chimney

мор

mor

closet

чулан

chulan

computer

компьютер

komp'iuter

couch

кушетка

kushetka

crib

бешик

beshik

cupboard

буфет

bufet

curtain

көшөгө/парда

köshögö/parda

desk

стол

stol

dining room

ашкана

ashkana

dishwasher

идиш жуугуч машине

idish juuguch mashine

door

эшик

eshik

---

driveway

кире бериш жол

kire berish jol

---

exterior

тышы/сырты

tyshy/syrty

---

family room

жалпы бөлмө

jalpy bölmö

---

fence

корук

koruk

---

fireplace

коломто

kolomto

---

floor

пол/каб**ат**

pol/kabat

---

foundation

пайдуб**ал**

payidubal

---

frame

алк**ак**

alkak

---

furniture

эмер**ек**

emerek

---

garage

гар**аж**

garaj

---

garden

бак/бак**ча**

bak/bakcha

---

hall/hallway

холл/оозгу үй

holl/oozgu üyi

insulation

изоляция/жылуулоо

izolyatziya/jyluuloo

kitchen

ашкана/ашүй

ashkana/ashüyi

laundry

кир жуугуч

kir juuguch

lawn

көкмайсан

kökmayisan

lawnmower

көкмайсан чапкыч

kökmayisan chapkych

library

китепкана

kitepkana

light

жарык

jaryk

living room

конок бөлмө

konok bölmö

lock

кулпу

kulpu

loft

чатыр асты/үстүңкү кабат

chatyr asty/üstüngkü kabat

mailbox

почта кутусу

pochta kutusu

mantle

жабуу/мантия

jabuu/mantiya

master bedroom

негизги уйку бөлмө

negizgi uyiku bölmö

neighborhood

конуш

konush

office

кеңсе/офис

kengse/ofis

pantry

чыгдан

chygdan

patio

терасса

terassa

plumbing

суу куурлар**ы**

suu kuurlary

---

pool

басс**е**йн

basseyin

---

porch

босог**о**

bosogo

---

roof

чат**ы**р

chatyr

---

shed

короо жай

koroo jayi

---

shelf/shelves

текч**е**/текчел**е**р

tekche/tekcheler

---

shingles

чат**ы**р бастырыг**ы**

chatyr bastyrygy

shower

чайнм**а**

chayiynma

shutters

калкалам**а**

kalkalama

siding

капто**о**

kaptoo

sofa

див**а**н/такт**а**

divan/takta

stairs/staircase

тепк**и**ч/шат**ы**

tepkich/shaty

telephone

телефон

telefon

television

телевизор

televizor

toilet

туалет/даараткана

tualet/daaratkana

wall

дубал

dubal

welcome mat

килемче

kilemche

window

терезе

tereze

yard

короо/эшиктин алды

koroo/eshiktin aldy

Related Verbs

Тиешелүү этиштер

Tieshelüü etishter

---

to build

куруу

kuruu

---

to buy

сатып алуу

satyp aluu

---

to clean

тазалоо

tazaloo

---

to decorate

кооздоо/жасалгалоо

koozdoo/jasalgaloo

to leave

кетүү

ketüü

to move in

көчүп келүү/кирүү

köchüp kelüü/kirüü

to move out

көчүп чыгуу/көчүп кетүү

köchüp chyguu/köchüp ketüü

to renovate

ремонттоо/ремонт кылуу/жаңылоо

remonttoo/remont kyluu/jangyloo

to repair

оңдоо

ongdoo

to sell

сатуу

satuu

to visit

конокко баруу/баруу

konokko baruu/baruu

9) Arts & Entertainment
9) Чеберчилик жана көңүл ачуу
9) Cheberchilik jana köngül achuu

3-D

3-D/3 өлчөмдүү

3-D/3 ölchömdüü

action

иш-чара

ish-chara

actor/actress

актёр/актриса/аткаруучу

aktyor/aktrisa/atkaruuchu

album

альбом

al'bom

alternative

альтернатива

al'ternativa

amphitheater

амфитеатр

amfiteatr

animation

анимация

animatziya

artist

сүрөтчү/устат

sürötchü/ustat

audience

аудитория/көрүүчүлөр/угуучулар

auditoriya/körüüchülör/uguuchular

ballet

балет

balet

band

топ/ансамбль

top/ansambl'

blues

блюз

bliuz

cast

курам/актёрлор ансамбли

kuram/aktyorlor ansambli

choreographer

хореограф

horeograf

cinema

кинотеатр

kinoteatr

comedy

комедия

komediya

commercial

жарнама/жарнама клип

jarnama/jarnama klip

composer

композитор

kompozitor

concert

концерт

kontzert

conductor

дирижёр

dirijyor

country

кантри

kantri

dance

бий

biyi

director

режиссёр

rejissyor

documentary

документтик фильм/документалдык фильм

dokumenttik fil'm/dokumentaldyk fil'm

---

drama

драма/трагедия

drama/tragediya

---

drummer

добулбасчы/доолбасчы

dobulbaschy/doolbaschy

---

duet

дуэт

duet

---

episode

эпизод/интермедия

epizod/intermediya

---

event

окуя/акт

okuya/akt

exhibition

көргөзмө

körgözmö

fantasy

фэнтези

fentezi

film

фильм

fil'm

genre

жанр

janr

group

топ

top

guitar

гитара

gitara

hip-hop

хип-хоп

hip-hop

horror

коркунучтуу

korkunuchtuu

inspirational

эргитүүчү

ergitüüchü

legend

уламыш/легенда

ulamysh/legenda

lyrics

лирика/лирикалык ырлар/сөздөр

lirika/lirikalyk yrlar/sözdör

magician

сыйкырчы

syyikyrchy

microphone

микрофон

mikrofon

motion picture

фильм/кино/тасма

fil'm/kino/tasma

museum

музей

muzeyi

music

музыка

muzyka

musical

мюзикл

miuzikl

musician

музыкант

muzykant

mystery

мистика/сырдуу окуя

mistika/syrduu okuya

opera

опера

opera

orchestra

оркестр

orkestr

painter

сүрөтчү

sürötchü

painting

сүрөт

süröt

performance

спектакль

spektakl'

play

пьеса

p'esa

---

producer

продюсер

prodiuser

---

rap

рэп

rep

---

repertoire

репертуар

repertuar

---

rock

рок

rok

---

romance

романтика/романтикалуу окуя

romantika/romantikaluu okuya

scene

декорация/окуя болгон жай/көшөгө

dekoratziya/okuya bolgon jayi/köshögö

science fiction

фантастика

fantastika

sculptor

скульптор

skul'ptor

singer

ырчы

yrchy

sitcom

ситком/ситуациялык комедия/жагдайлык комедия

sitkom/situatziyalyk komediya/jagdayilyk komediya

song

ыр

yr

songwriter

ырдын автору/ыр жазуучу

yrdyn avtoru/yr jazuuchu

stage

сахна

sahna

stand-up comedy

стенд-ап комедия

stend-ap komediya

television

телекөрсөтүү

telekörsötüü

theater

театр

teatr

understudy

дублёр/экинчи курамдагы актёр

dublyor/ekinchi kuramdagy aktyor

Related Verbs

Тиешелүү этиштер

Tieshelüü etishter

to act

аткаруу

atkaruu

to applaud

кол чабуу

kol chabuu

to conduct

жетектөө/дирижёрлоо

jetektöö/dirijyorloo

to dance

бийлөө

biyilöö

to direct

жетектөө/башкаруу

jetektöö/bashkaruu

to draw

тартуу

tartuu

---

to entertain

коноктоо/көңүл ачуу

konoktoo/köngül achuu

---

to host

алып баруу/өткөрүү

alyp baruu/ötkörüü

---

to paint

тартуу

tartuu

---

to perform

аткаруу

atkaruu

---

to play

ойноо/аткаруу

oyinoo/atkaruu

---

to show

көрсөтүү

körsötüü

to sing

ырдоо

yrdoo

to star

башкы ролду ойноо

bashky roldu oyinoo

to watch

көрүү

körüü

10) Games and Sports
10) Оюндар жана спорт
10) Oiundar jana sport

amateur

сүйүүчү

süyiüüchü

---

arena

арена/секи/талаа

arena/seki/talaa

---

ball

топ

top

---

baseball

бейсбол

beyisbol

---

basketball

баскетбол

basketbol

---

bicycle

велосип**е**д

*velosip**e**d*

bowling

б**о**улинг

*b**o**uling*

boxing

бокс

boks

championship

чемпион**а**т

*chempion**a**t*

competition

атаандашт**ы**к/мелд**е**ш

*ataandasht**y**k/meld**e**sh*

course

а**я**нт/тала**а**/аянтч**а**

*a**y**ant/tala**a**/ayantch**a***

court

оюн аянты

oiun ayanty

defense

коргоо

korgoo

equestrian

чабарман

chabarman

event

окуя/иш-чара

okuya/ish-chara

fan

күйөрман

küyiörman

fencing

чабышуу

chabyshuu

field

аянт/талаа

ayant/talaa

---

football

футбол

futbol

---

gear

форма/шайман

forma/shayiman

---

goal

гол

gol

---

golf

гольф

gol'f

---

gym

машыгуу залы/спорт зал

mashyguu zaly/sport zal

---

gymnastics

гимнастика

gimnastika

halftime

таймдар арасындагы тыныгуу

tayimdar arasyndagy tynyguu

helmet

туулга

tuulga

hockey

хоккей

hokkeyi

ice skating

кырчаңгы тебүү

kyrchanggy tebüü

league

лига

liga

martial arts

согуш өнөрлөрү

sogush önörlörü

match

матч

match

medal

медаль

medal'

offense

чабуул

chabuul

Olympic Games

Олимпиада оюндары

Olimpiada oiundary

pentathlon

пентатлон

pentatlon

play

беру́у/пас беру́у

berüü/pas berüü

player

каарман/оюнчу

kaarman/oiunchu

professional

кесипкөй

kesipköyi

puck

шайба

shayiba

quarter

чейрек

cheyirek

race

жарыш

jarysh

record

рекорд

rekord

---

referee

рефери

referi

---

riding

ат чабыш

at chabysh

---

ring

ринг

ring

---

rink

муз майдан/муз аянт

muz mayidan/muz ayant

---

running

чуркоо

churkoo

---

score

упай

upayi

skiing

чаңгы спорт

changgy sport

soccer

футбол

futbol

softball

софтбол

softbol

spectators

көрүүчүлөр

körüüchülör

sport

спорт

sport

sportsmanship

спорттук беделдүүлүк

sporttuk bedeldüülük

stadium

стадион

stadion

swimming

сүзүү/чабак уруу

süzüü/chabak uruu

team

тайпа

tayipa

tennis

теннис

tennis

track and field

жеңил атлетика

jengil atletika

volleyball

воллейбол

volleyibol

---

winner

жеңүүчү/утуучу

jengüüchü/utuuchu

---

wrestling

күрөш

kürösh

Related Verbs

Тиешелүү этиштер

Tieshelüü etishter

to cheat

алдоо/буйдамалоо/митаамдык кылуу

aldoo/buyidamaloo/mitaamdyk kyluu

---

to compete

атаандашуу/таймашуу

ataandashuu/tayimashuu

---

to dribble

топту алып баруу

toptu alyp baruu

to go

баруу/жүрүү

baruu/jürüü

to lose

утулуу/жоготуу/алдыруу

utuluu/jogotuu/aldyruu

to play

ойноо

oyinoo

to race

жарышуу

jaryshuu

to score

упай алуу/гол киргизүү

upayi aluu/gol kirgizüü

to win

утуу/жеңүү

utuu/jengüü

11) Food
11) Тамак
11) Tamak

apple

алма

alma

---

bacon

бекон

bekon

---

banana

банан

banan

---

beans

буурчак

buurchak

---

beef

уй эти

uyi eti

---

bread

нан

nan

brownie

шоколаддуу кекс

shokoladduu keks

cake

пирог

pirog

candy

момпосуй

momposuyi

carrot

сабиз

sabiz

celery

сельдерей

sel'dereyi

cheese

сыр/быштак

syr/byshtak

chicken

тоок эти

took eti

chocolate

шоколад

shokolad

cookie

печенье

pechen'e

crackers

крекер

kreker

fish

балык

balyk

fruit

мөмө/жемиш

mömö/jemish

ham

ветчина

vetchina

herbs

дары чөп

dary chöp

honey

бал

bal

ice cream

бал муздак

bal muzdak

jelly/jam

варенье

varen'e

ketchup

кетчуп

ketchup

---

lemon

лимон

limon

---

lettuce

латук

latuk

---

mayonnaise

майонез

mayionez

---

meat

эт

et

---

melon

коон

koon

---

milk

сүт

süt

mustard

горчица/сары кычы

gorchitza/sary kychy

nuts

жаңгактар

janggaktar

orange

апельсин

apel'sin

pasta

түтүк кесме

tütük kesme

pastry

кондитердик даам-татымдар

konditerdik daam-tatymdar

pepper

калемп**и**р

kalempir

pork

чочк**о** эти

chochko eti

potato

карт**о**шка/карт**ө**шк**ө**

kartoshka/kartöshkö

salad

сал**ат**

salat

sandwich

с**е**ндвич

sendvich

sausage

колбас**а**/чуч**у**к

kolbasa/chuchuk

soup

сорп**о**/шорп**о**

sorpo/shorpo

spice

курчутм**а** татым**а**л

kurchutma tatymal

steak

стейк

steyik

strawberry

кулпун**ай**

kulpunayi

sugar

кант/шек**е**р/кум-шек**е**р

kant/sheker/kum-sheker

tea

чай

chayi

toast

ТОСТ

tost

---

tomato

томат/помидор

tomat/pomidor

---

vegetables

жашылчалар

jashylchalar

---

water

суу

suu

---

wheat

буудай

buudayi

Restaurants and Cafes

Ресторандар жана кафелер

Restorandar jana kafeler

a la carte

өзүнчө/меню боюнча

özünchö/meniu boiuncha

---

a la mode

бал муздак менен

bal muzdak menen

---

appetizer

ысылык

ysylyk

---

bar

бар

bar

---

beverage

суусундук

suusunduk

---

bill

дүмүрчөк/эсеп

dümürchök/esep

bistro

бистро

bistro

breakfast

эртең мененки тамак/таңкы тамак

erteng menenki tamak/tangky tamak

brunch

бранч

branch

cafe/cafeteria

кафе/кафетерий

kafe/kafeteriyi

cashier

кассир

kassir

chair

отургуч

oturguch

charge

төлөм

tölöm

check

чек

chek

chef

башкы ашпозчу

bashky ashpozchu

condiments

татымалдар

tatymaldar

cook

ашпозчу

ashpozchu

deli/delicatessen

муздак татымалдар

muzdak tatymaldar

dessert

десерт

desert

diner

кафе-ашкана/буфет

kafe-ashkana/bufet

dinner

тамак/тамактануу

tamak/tamaktanuu

dishwasher

идиш жуугуч

idish juuguch

doggie bag

баштык

bashtyk

drink

ичимдик

ichimdik

---

entree

негизги тамак

negizgi tamak

---

food

тамак

tamak

---

gourmet

гурман/гастроном

gurman/gastronom

---

hor d'oeuvre

чүйгүн

chüyigün

---

host/hostess

кожоюн

kojoiun

---

lunch

ланч

lanch

manager

м**е**нежер

menejer

menu

мен**ю**

meniu

party

кеч**е**

keche

platter

чоң табак

chong tabak

reservation

ээлөө

eelöö

restaurant

ресторан

restoran

---

server/waiter/waitress

официант

ofitziant

---

silverware

күмүш идиш

kümüsh idish

---

table

стол

stol

---

tip

чайпул

chayipul

---

to go

баруу

baruu

Related Verbs

Тиешелүү этиштер
Tieshelüü etishter

to bake

бышыруу

byshyruu

___

to be hungry

ачка болуу

achka boluu

___

to cook

бышыруу

byshyruu

___

to cut

кесүү

kesüü

___

to dine

тамактануу

tamaktanuu

___

to drink

ичүү

ichüü

to eat

тамактануу/же

tamaktanuu/je

to eat out

үйдөн тышкары тамактануу

üyidön tyshkary tamaktanuu

to grow

өсүү

ösüü

to have breakfast/lunch/dinner

түшкө чейинки/түштөн кийинки/кечки тамак же

tüshkö cheyiinki/tüshtön kiyiinki/kechki tamak je

to order

тапшырык берүү

tapshyryk berüü

to pay

төлөө

tölöö

---

to prepare

тамак жасоо

tamak jasoo

---

to reserve

ээлеп коюу

eelep koiuu

---

to serve

берүү

berüü

---

to taste

татуу/даамдануу

tatuu/daamdanuu

12) Shopping
12) Дүкөнчүлөө
12) Dükönchülöö

bags

баштыктар

bashtyktar

barcode

штрих-код

shtrih-kod

basket

себет

sebet

bookstore

китеп дүкөнү

kitep dükönü

boutique

бутик

butik

browse

аралоо

araloo

buggy/shopping cart

дүкөнчүлөө арабасы

dükönchülöö arabasy

butcher

касапчы

kasapchy

cash

нак акча

nak akcha

cashier

кассир

kassir

change

кайтарым

kayitarym

changing room

кийинүү бөлмөсү

kiyiinüü bölmösü

check

чек

chek

clearance

сатып түгөтүү

satyp tügötüü

convenience store

күнү-түнү иштеген дүкөн

künü-tünü ishtegen dükön

credit card

кредиттик карта

kredittik karta

customer

кардар

kardar

debit card

дебеттик карта

debettik karta

delivery

жеткизүү

jetkizüü

department store

универсалдык дүкөн

universaldyk dükön

discount

жеңилдик

jengildik

drugstore/pharmacy

аптека/дарыкана

apteka/darykana

escalator

эскалатор

eskalator

florist

флорист

florist

---

grocery

азык-түлүк

azyk-tülük

---

hardware

эмгек куралдары

emgek kuraldary

---

jeweler

зергер

zerger

---

mall

соода борбору

sooda borboru

---

market

базар

bazar

---

receipt

дүмүрчөк

dümürchök

---

return

кайтаруу

kayitaruu

---

sale

арзандатуу

arzandatuu

---

salesman

сатуучу

satuuchu

---

size

өлчөм

ölchöm

---

shoe store

чокой дүкөн

chokoyi dükön

---

shopping center

соода жана көңүл ачуу борбору

sooda jana köngül achuu borboru

---

store

дүкөн

dükön

---

supermarket

супермаркет

supermarket

---

wholesale

дүң

düng

Related Verbs

Тиешелүү этиштер

Tieshelüü etishter

to buy

сатып алуу

satyp aluu

---

to charge

төлөтүү

tölötüü

---

to exchange

алмаштыруу

almashtyruu

---

to return

кайтаруу/кайтарып берүү

kayitaruu/kayitaryp berüü

---

to save

сактоо

saktoo

---

to sell

сатуу

satuu

---

to shop

дүкөнчүлөө

dükönchülöö

---

to spend

сарпто**о**/коротуу

sarptoo/korotuu

to try on

кий**и**п көрүү

kiyiip körüü

13) At the Bank
13) Банкта
13) Bankta

account

эсеп

esep

___

APR

жылдык проценттик өлчөм

jyldyk protzenttik ölchöm

___

ATM

банкомат

bankomat

___

balance

баланс

balans

___

bank

банк

bank

___

borrower

насыя алуучу/кредит алуучу

nasyya aluuchu/kredit aluuchu

bounced check

жабылбаган чек/кайтарылган чек

jabylbagan chek/kayitarylgan chek

cash

нак акча

nak akcha

check

чек

chek

checkbook

чектер китепчеси

chekter kitepchesi

checking account

чектик эсеп

chektik esep

collateral

күрөөлүк мүлк

küröölük mülk

credit

насыя/кредит

nasyya/kredit

credit card

кредиттик карта

kredittik karta

credit limit

кредиттик лимит

kredittik limit

credit rating

кредиттик рейтинг

kredittik reyiting

currency

валюта

valiuta

debt

карыз

karyz

---

debit

дебет

debet

---

debit card

дебеттик карта

debettik karta

---

deposit

депозит

depozit

---

fees

төлөмдөр

tölömdör

---

interest

проценттик өлчөм

protzenttik ölchöm

---

loan

карыз/кредит/насыя

karyz/kredit/nasyya

money

акча

akcha

money market

акча базары

akcha bazary

mortgage

кыймылсыз мүлк

kyyimylsyz mülk

NSF

акча каражат менен жабылбаган вексель

akcha karajat menen jabylbagan veksel'

overdraft

овердрафт

overdraft

payee

төлөм алуучу

tölöm aluuchu

PIN

жеке идентификациялык номур/PIN

jeke identifikatziyalyk nomur/PIN

---

register

реестр/китеп/журнал

reestr/kitep/jurnal

---

savings account

топтолмо эсеп

toptolmo esep

---

statement

банк эсебинин көчүрмөсү

bank esebinin köchürmösü

---

telebanking

телебанкинг

telebanking

---

teller

банк кызматкер**и**

bank kyzmatkeri

---

transaction

транз**а**кция

tranzaktziya

---

traveler's check

жол чег**и**

jol chegi

---

withdraw

эсепт**е**н чыгару**у**

esepten chygaruu

Related Verbs

Тиешелүү этиштер

Tieshelüü etishter

to borrow

карызг**а** алу**у**

karyzga aluu

---

to cash

акчан**ы** накталату**у**

akchany naktalatuu

to charge

төлөт**үү**

tölötüü

to deposit

депозитк**е** салу**у**

depozitke saluu

to endorse

ырасто**о**

yrastoo

to hold

кармо**о**

karmoo

to lend

карызг**а** бер**үү**

karyzga berüü

to open an account

эсеп ачуу

esep achuu

---

to pay

төлөө

tölöö

---

to save

сактоо

saktoo

---

to transfer money

акча которуу/акча жөнөтүү

akcha kotoruu/akcha jönötüü

---

to withdraw

акча чыгаруу/эсептен акча чыгаруу

akcha chygaruu/esepten akcha chygaruu

---

14) Holidays
14) Майрамдар
14) Mayiramdar

celebration

майрамдо**о**

mayiramdoo

decorations

кооздоол**о**р

koozdoolor

federal

федералд**ы**к

federaldyk

festivities

майрамд**ы**к иш-чарал**а**р

mayiramdyk ish-charalar

fireworks

фейерверкт**е**р

feyierverkter

gifts

белект**е**р

belekter

heroes

каарманд**а**р

kaarmandar

national

улутт**у**к

uluttuk

parade

пар**а**д

parad

party

кеч**е**

keche

picnics

пикникт**е**р

piknikter

resolution

сөз берүү

söz berüü

---

traditions

салттар

salttar

American Holidays in calendar order:

Американын майрамдарынын иреттелген тизмеги:

Amerikanyn mayiramdarynyn irettelgen tizmegi:

New Year's Day

Жаңы жыл

Jangy jyl

Valentine's Day

Валентин күнү

Valentin künü

St. Patrick's Day

Ыйык Патрик күнү

Yyiyk Patrik künü

Easter

Пасха

Pasha

Earth Day

Жер күнү

Jer künü

Mother's Day

Энелер күнү

Eneler künü

Memorial Day

Эскерүү күнү

Eskerüü künü

Father's Day

Аталар күнү

Atalar künü

Flag Day

Желек күнү

Jelek künü

Independence Day

Көз карандысыздык күнү

Köz karandysyzdyk künü

Labor Day

Эмгек күнү

Emgek künü

Halloween

Хэллоуин

Hellouin

Veteran's Day

Ветерандар күнү

Veterandar künü

Thanksgiving Day

Алкыш айтуу күнү

Alkysh ayituu künü

Christmas

Рождество

Rojdestvo

Hanukkah

Ханука

Hanuka

New Year's Eve

Жаң**ы** жылд**ы** тосу**у**

Jangy jyldy tosuu

Related Verbs

Тиешелүү этиштер
Tieshelüü etishter

to celebrate

майрамдо**о**

mayiramdoo

---

to commemorate

эскерү**ү**

eskerüü

---

to give

берү**ү**

berüü

---

to honor

арноо

arnoo

to observe

сактоо/тутуу

saktoo/tutuu

to party

сайрандоо

sayirandoo

to recognize

таануу

taanuu

to remember

эскерүү

eskerüü

15) Traveling
15) Саякаттоо
15) Sayakattoo

airport

аэропорт/аба майдан

aeroport/aba mayidan

baggage

багаж/жүк

bagaj/jük

boarding pass

отургузуу талону

oturguzuu talonu

business class

бизнес класс

biznes klass

bus station

автобекет

avtobeket

carry-on

кол-жүк

kol-jük

coach

вагон

vagon

cruise

круиз

kruiz

depart/departure

учуп чыгуу/кетүү

uchup chyguu/ketüü

destination

көздөө жайы

közdöö jayiy

first class

биринчи класс

birinchi klass

flight

учуу

uchuu

flight attendant

борт коштоочу

bort koshtoochu

luggage

жүк

jük

map

карта

karta

passenger

пассажир/жүргүнчү

passajir/jürgünchü

passport

паспорт

pasport

pilot

пилот

pilot

postcard

почта картасы

pochta kartasy

rail

рельс

rel's

red-eye

түнкү рейс

tünkü reyis

reservations

ээлөөлөр

eelöölör

road

жол

jol

sail

кеме

keme

---

seat

орун

orun

---

sightseeing

экскурсия

ekskursiya

---

souvenir

сувенир/азембелек

suvenir/azembelek

---

suitcase

чемодан

chemodan

---

tour

тур

tur

---

tourist

турист

turist

travel

саякат

sayakat

travel agent

саякат агенти

sayakat agenti

trip

сапар

sapar

vacation

өргүү/дем алыш

örgüü/dem alysh

Modes of Transportation

Транспорттун түрлөрү

Transporttun türlörü

Airplane/plane

Учак

Uchak

---

automobile

автомобиль/машине

avtomobil'/mashine

---

boat

кайык

kayiyk

---

bus

автобус

avtobus

---

car

машине

mashine

---

ferry

паром

parom

motorcycle

мотоцикл

mototzikl

motor home

унаа үй

unaa üyi

ship

кеме

keme

subway

метро

metro

taxi

такси

taksi

train

поезд

poezd

---

truck

жүк унаа

jük unaa

Hotels

Мейманканалар
Meyimankanalar

airport shuttle

аэропорттун автобусу

aeroporttun avtobusu

---

all-inclusive

бардыгы кошулган

bardygy koshulgan

---

amenities

тиричилик ыңгайлуулуктары

tirichilik ynggayiluuluktary

---

balcony

балкон

balkon

bathroom

ванна

vanna

beds

керебеттер

kerebetter

bed and breakfast

таңкы тамагы камтылган бөлмө

tangky tamagy kamtylgan bölmö

bellboy/bellhop

мейманкананын чабарманы/чабарман

meyimankananyn chabarmany/chabarman

bill

эсеп

esep

business center

бизнес борбор

biznes borbor

cable/satellite TV

кабелдик/спутниктик телекөрсөтүү

kabeldik/sputniktik telekörsötüü

charges (in-room)

(бөлмө ичиндеги) сарптоолор

(bölmö ichindegi) sarptoolor

concierge

консьерж/вахтачы

kons'erj/vahtachy

elevator

элеватор/лифт

elevator/lift

exercise/fitness room

көнүгүү/машыгуу бөлмөсү

könügüü/mashyguu bölmösü

front desk

каттоо

kattoo

---

gift shop

белектер дүкөнү

belekter dükönü

---

guest

конок

konok

---

high-rise

көп кабаттуу

köp kabattuu

---

hotel

мейманкана/отель

meyimankana/otel'

---

housekeeping

бөлмөлөрдү тазалоо кызматы

bölmölördü tazaloo kyzmaty

---

inn

конок үй

konok üyi

key

ачкыч

achkych

lobby

холл/вестибюль

holl/vestibiul'

lounge

фойе

foyie

luxury

люкс

liuks

maid

үй кызматкер айым

üyi kyzmatker ayiym

manager

менежер

menejer

---

meeting room

жолугушуу бөлмөсү

jolugushuu bölmösü

---

mini-bar

мини бар

mini bar

---

motel

мотель

motel'

---

non-smoking

чылым чекпегендер үчүн

chylym chekpegender üchün

---

pool - indoor/outdoor

ички/тышкы бассейн

ichki/tyshky basseyin

---

parking

автотурук

avtoturuk

reception desk

каттоо кабылдамасы

kattoo kabyldamasy

reservation

ээлөө

eelöö

resort

пансионат/эс алуу комплекси

pansionat/es aluu kompleksi

restaurant

ресторан

restoran

room number

бөлмө номуру

bölmö nomuru

room service

бөлмө кызматы

bölmö kyzmaty

service charge

тейлөө наркы

teyilöö narky

suite

уктоо жана жалпы бөлмөлөрү бар номур

uktoo jana jalpy bölmölörü bar nomur

vacancy

бош орун

bosh orun

Related Verbs

Тиешелүү этиштер
Tieshelüü etishter

to arrive

келүү

kelüü

to buy

сатып алуу

satyp aluu

to change

алмаштыруу

almashtyruu

to check-in/out

кирүү/чыгуу

kirüü/chyguu

to drive

айдоо

ayidoo

to fly

учуу

uchuu

to land

кондуруу/конуу

konduruu/konuu

to make a reservation

ээлөө

eelöö

---

to pack

салыштыруу

salyshtyruu

---

to pay

төлөө

tölöö

---

to rent

ижарага алуу

ijaraga aluu

---

to see

көрүү

körüü

---

to stay

калуу/жайгашуу

kaluu/jayigashuu

---

to take off

учуп чыгуу

uchup chyguu

to travel

саякаттоо

sayakattoo

16) School
16) Мектеп
16) Mektep

assignment

тапшырма

tapshyrma

---

backpack

рюкзак

riukzak

---

book

китеп

kitep

---

book bag

китеп баштык

kitep bashtyk

---

calculator

калкулятор

kalkulyator

---

calendar

календарь/күнбарак

kalendar'/künbarak

---

chalk

бор

bor

---

chalkboard

бор такта

bor takta

---

chart

күн тартиби

kün tartibi

---

class

класс

klass

---

classmate

классташ

klasstash

classroom

класс

klass

---

colored pencils

түстүү карандаштар

tüstüü karandashtar

---

computer

компьютер

komp'iuter

---

construction paper

калың түстүү кагаз

kalyng tüstüü kagaz

---

crayons

түстүү борлор/түстүү карандаштар

tüstüü borlor/tüstüü karandashtar

---

desk

парта

parta

---

dictionary

сөздүк

sözdük

diploma

диплом

diplom

dormitory

жатакана

jatakana

encyclopedia

энциклопедия

entziklopediya

English

Англис тили

Anglis tili

eraser

өчүргүч

öchürgüch

exam

экзамен

ekzamen

experiment

эксперимент

eksperiment

geography

география

geografiya

globe

глобус

globus

glue

желим/клей

jelim/kleyi

grades (A,B,C,D,F)

баалар (5,4,3,2,1)

baalar (5,4,3,2,1)

gym

спорт зал

sport zal

headmaster

мектеп**т**ин директор**у**

mekteptin direktoru

history

тар**ы**х

taryh

homework

үй тапшырм**а**

üyi tapshyrma

lesson

сабак

sabak

library

китепкан**а**

kitepkana

lockers

жеке кулпуланма **я**щик/**я**щик

jeke kulpulanma yash'ik/yash'ik

lunch box/bag

там**а**к салг**ы**ч конт**е**йнер/там**а**к салг**ы**ч башт**ы**к

tamak salgych konteyiner/tamak salgych bashtyk

map

к**а**рта

karta

markers

фломастерл**е**р/маркерл**е**р

flomasterler/markerler

math

матем**а**тика

matematika

notebook

блокн**о**т/жандепт**е**р

bloknot/jandepter

paper

кагаз

kagaz

pen

калемсап

kalemsap

pencil

карандаш

karandash

pencil sharpener

учтагыч

uchtagych

physical education/PE

дене тарбия

dene tarbiya

portfolio

портфель/папка

portfel'/papka

principal

мектептин директору

mekteptin direktoru

professor

профессор

professor

project

проект/долбоор

proekt/dolboor

quiz

текшерүү иш

teksherüü ish

reading

окуу

okuu

recess

танапис

tanapis

ruler

сызгыч

syzgych

science

илим

ilim

scissors

кайчы

kayichy

semester

семестр

semestr

student

студент/окуучу

student/okuuchu

teacher

мугалим/окутуучу

mugalim/okutuuchu

test

тест/текшерүү

test/teksherüü

thesaurus

тезаурус

tezaurus

vocabulary

сөз байлыгы

söz bayilygy

Related Verbs

Тиешелүү этиштер
Tieshelüü etishter

to answer

жооп берүү

joop berüü

to ask

суроо

suroo

to drop out

чыг**ы**п калу**у**

*chyg**y**p kalu**u***

---

to fail

о**ң**ун**а**н чыкп**оо**

*ongun**a**n chykp**oo***

---

to learn

үйр**ө**н**үү**

*üyir**ö**n**üü***

---

to pass

өт**үү**

*öt**üü***

---

to play

ойн**оо**

*oyin**oo***

---

to read

ок**уу**

*ok**uu***

---

to register

катталуу

kattaluu

to study

окуу

okuu

to teach

сабак берүү/үйрөтүү

sabak berüü/üyirötüü

to test

текшерүү

teksherüü

to think

ойлонуу

oyilonuu

to write

жазуу

jazuu

17) Hospital
17) Оорукана
17) Oorukana

allergy/allergic

аллергия/аллергик

allergiya/allergik

amnesia

амнезия/эс-тутумун жоготуу

amneziya/es-tutumun jogotuu

amputation

ампутация

amputatziya

anesthesiologist

анестезиолог

anesteziolog

antibiotics

антибиотиктер

antibiotikter

appointment

жазылуу

jazyluu

asthma

астма

astma

bacteria

бактерия

bakteriya

biopsy

биопсия

biopsiya

blood

кан

kan

blood donor

кан донору

kan donoru

blood pressure

кан басым**ы**

kan basymy

blood test

канд**ы** текшерүү

kandy teksherüü

bone

сөөк

söök

brace

бандаж/корсет/шина/ортодонттук кашаа

bandaj/korset/shina/ortodonttuk kashaa

bruise

урунган жер

urungan jer

C-section

кесардык кесүү

kesardyk kesüü

cancer

чаян оору/рак

chayan ooru/rak

CPR

жүрөк-өпкөлүк реанимация

jürök-öpkölük reanimatziya

cast

цилиндрлер

tzilindrler

chemotherapy

химиотерапия

himioterapiya

coroner

коронер

koroner

critical

критикалык/оор

kritikalyk/oor

crutches

балдак

baldak

---

deficiency

дефект/жетишпестик

defekt/jetishpestik

---

dehydrated

суусуздандырылган

suusuzdandyrylgan

---

diabetes

диабет

diabet

---

diagnosis

диагноз

diagnoz

---

disease

оору

ooru

---

doctor

доктур/дарыгер

doktur/daryger

ER

реаниматология

reanimatologiya

exam

изилдөө/текшерүү

izildöö/teksherüü

fever

ысытма

ysytma

flu

сасык тумоо/грипп

sasyk tumoo/gripp

fracture

сынык/сынуу

synyk/synuu

heart attack

жүрөк туталагы

jürök tutalagy

hives

бөрү жатыш

börü jatysh

illness

оору

ooru

imaging

визуалдаштыруу

vizualdashtyruu

immunization

вакцинация

vaktzinatziya

infection

инфекция

infektziya

ICU

реанимациялык палата

reanimatziyalyk palata

IV

венанын ичине

venanyn ichine

laboratory

лаборатория

laboratoriya

life support

тиричиликти колдоо

tirichilikti koldoo

mass

шишик

shishik

medical technician

медициналык техник

meditzinalyk tehnik

nurse

медайым/медициналык айым

medayiym/meditzinalyk ayiym

OR

операциялык палата

operatziyalyk palata

operation

операция

operatziya

orthopedic

ортопедиялык/протездөөчү

ortopediyalyk/protezdÖÖchü

pain

оору/сыздоо

ooru/syzdoo

patient

пациент

patzient

pediatrician

педиатр

pediatr

pharmacy

фармацевтика

farmatzevtika

physician

терапевт

terapevt

prescription

рецепт

retzept

psychiatrist

психиатр

psihiatr

radiologist

рентгенолог

rentgenolog

resident

ординатор/интерн

ordinator/intern

---

scan

томография

tomografiya

---

shot

ийне атуу

iyine atuu

---

side effects

кыйыр таасирлер

kyyiyr taasirler

---

specialist

специалист

spetzialist

---

stable

туруктуу

turuktuu

---

surgeon

хирург

hirurg

symptoms

симптомдор

simptomdor

therapy

терапия

terapiya

treatment

дарылоо

daryloo

visiting hours

кабыл алуу сааттары

kabyl aluu saattary

wheelchair

отургуч-араба

oturguch-araba

x-ray

рентген

rentgen

Related Verbs

Тиешелүү этиштер
Tieshelüü etishter

to cough

жөтөлүү

jötölüü

---

to examine

изилдөө/текшерүү

izildöö/teksherüü

---

to feel

сезүү

sezüü

---

to give

берүү

berüü

---

to hurt

ооруу

ooruu

---

to prescribe

рецепт жазып берүү

retzept jazyp berüü

---

to scan

томографиядан өткөрүү

tomografiyadan ötkörüü

---

to take

алуу/ичүү

aluu/ichüü

---

to test

текшерүү

teksherüü

---

to treat

дарылоо

daryloo

---

to visit

баруу

baruu

to wait

күтүү

kütüü

18) Emergency
18) Кырсыктар
18) Kyrsyktar

accident

кокустук

kokustuk

ambulance

тез жардам унаасы

tez jardam unaasy

blizzard

бурганак/бороон

burganak/boroon

blood/bleeding

кан/каноо

kan/kanoo

broken bone

сынган сөөк

syngan söök

chest pain

көкүрөктөгү оору

kökuröktögü ooru

choking

чачоо/какоо

chachoo/kakoo

coast guard

жээк сакчылары

jeek sakchylary

crash

талкалануу/кыйроо

talkalanuu/kyyiroo

drowning

чөгүү

chögüü

earthquake

жер титирөө/жер силкинүү

jer titiröö/jer silkinüü

emergency

авария/өзгөчө учур

avariya/özgöchö uchur

EMT

өзгөчө учурлар боюнча медициналык
техник

özgöchö uchurlar boiuncha meditzinalyk tehnik

explosion

жарылуу/жардыруу

jaryluu/jardyruu

fight

койгулашуу/кагышуу

koyigulashuu/kagyshuu

fire

өрт

ört

fire department

өрт өчүрүүчүлөр

ört öchürüüchülör

fire escape

өрт учурунда чыгуучу жол

ört uchurunda chyguuchu jol

firefighter

өрт өчүргүч

ört öchürgüch

fire truck

өрт өчүргүч унаа

ört öchürgüch unaa

first aid

биринчи жардам

birinchi jardam

flood

сел/ташкын

sel/tashkyn

gun

ок атуучу курал

ok atuuchu kural

heart attack

жүрөк туталагы

jürök tutalagy

Heimlich maneuver

Хеймлих ыкмасы

Heyimlih ykmasy

---

help

жардам

jardam

---

hospital

оорукана/госпиталь

oorukana/gospital'

---

hurricane

бороон-чапкын

boroon-chapkyn

---

injury

жаракат

jarakat

---

ladder

тепк**ич**/шат**ы**

tepkich/shaty

lifeguard

жансакч**ы**/куткарг**ы**ч

jansakchy/kutkargych

life support

тиричиликт**и** колдо**о**

tirichilikti koldoo

lost

жоголг**о**н

jogolgon

natural disaster

жаратыл**ы**ш кырсыг**ы**

jaratylysh kyrsygy

officer

офиц**е**р

ofitzer

poison

уу

uu

police

полиция/милиция

politziya/militziya

rescue

куткаруу

kutkaruu

robbery

тоноо/карактоо

tonoo/karaktoo

shooting

атышуу

atyshuu

storm

шторм

shtorm

stroke

инсульт

insul't

---

tornado

куюн

kuiun

---

unconscious

эсин жоготкон

esin jogotkon

Related Verbs

Тиешелүү этиштер
Tieshelüü etishter

to bleed

кансыроо

kansyroo

---

to break

сындырып алуу/сындыруу

syndyryp aluu/syndyruu

---

to breathe

дем алуу

dem aluu

to burn

күйгүзүп алуу

küyigüzüp aluu

to call

чакыруу/чалуу

chakyruu/chaluu

to crash

кыйроо/талкалануу

kyyiroo/talkalanuu

to cut

кесүү

kesüü

to escape

качуу

kachuu

to faint

алсыроо/баш айлануу

alsyroo/bash ayilanuu

to fall

жыгылуу

jygyluu

to help

жардам берүү

jardam berüü

to hurt

ооруу/сыздоо

ooruu/syzdoo

to rescue

куткаруу

kutkaruu

to save

сактап калуу

saktap kaluu

to shoot

атуу

atuu

---

to wreck

аварияга учуратуу/кыйроого алып келүү

avariyaga uchuratuu/kyyiroogo alyp kelüü

---

www.ingramcontent.com/pod-product-compliance
Lightning Source LLC
LaVergne TN
LVHW051623080426

835511LV00016B/2140